THIS JOURNAL BELONGS TO

....

DATE

....

The best reason to pray is that God is really there. In praying, our unbelief gradually starts to melt. God moves smack into the middle of even an ordinary day.... Prayer is a matter of keeping at it.... Thunderclaps and lightning flashes are very unlikely. It is well to start small and quietly.

Emily Griffin

You are a beautiful child of God, precious to Him in every way. As you seek Him, He will listen to the prayers of your heart and fill your quiet time with His peace. He will infuse your ordinary day with His presence and guidance and love.

We have gathered prayers, promises, and praises for those issues closest to your heart. Let this journal inspire you to record your personal prayers, express your thoughts, embrace your dreams, and listen to what God is saying to you.

The Editors

If you make yourselves at home with me and my words are at home in you, you can be sure that whatever you ask will be listened to and acted upon.

JOHN 15:7 MSG

Father, I abandon myself into Your hands;
Do with me what you will.
Whatever You may do, I thank You:
I am ready for all, I accept all.
Let only Your will be done in me.

Charles de Foucauld

Commit to the Lord whatever you do, and he will establish your plans.

PROVERBS 16:3 NIV

Lord, You have given me a desire to accomplish great things.
You have placed dreams in my heart. Make me worthy of the dreams
You have prepared. Open my mind to the possibilities and give me
the strength to do what needs to be done. Amen. MJ

No eye has seen, no ear has heard, and no mind has imagined
what God has prepared for those who love him.

1 CORINTHIANS 2:9 NLT

Dear Lord, show me Your favor,
At all times keep me blessed,
May Your face ever shine upon me,
With peace and perfect rest.
Amen.

Mary Fairchild

The LORD bless you and keep you; the LORD make His face shine upon you,
and be gracious to you; the LORD lift up His countenance upon you,
and give you peace.

NUMBERS 6:24–26 NKJV

$\mathcal{D}$ear Father, thank You for holding me in Your hands
no matter where I am. You amaze me. You have things
set in place before I even know I need them. Remind me today
that You are the One in charge of my plans. You have everything
under control. All I need to do is trust. Amen. MJ

"For I know the plans I have for you," says the LORD. "They are plans for good and not for disaster, to give you a future and a hope."

JEREMIAH 29:11 NLT

*L*ord, guide my life to good and beautiful things. Give me grace.
And help me to follow You all the days of my life. Amen.

Prayer from Psalm 23

The LORD will guide you continually,
And satisfy your soul in drought,
And strengthen your bones.

ISAIAH 58:11 NKJV

Lord, hear my prayer. When I stumble over my words, or when I can't find the right words to say, listen to my heart. I want to talk with You. I want to walk with You. Hear me, O Lord, and answer with grace and love and mercy. Take my hand and my heart and lead me in prayer. Amen. MJ

The Spirit helps us with our weakness. We do not know how to pray as we should.
But the Spirit himself speaks to God for us, even begs God for us
with deep feelings that words cannot explain.

ROMANS 8:26 NCV

....

....

....

....

....

....

....

....

....

....

....

....

....

....

....

....

....

....

....

....

Almighty God, thank You for the job of this day. May we find gladness in all its toil and difficulty, its pleasure and success, and even in its failure and sorrow.

Charles Lewis Slattery

We were crushed and overwhelmed beyond our ability to endure, and we thought we would never live through it. In fact, we expected to die. But as a result, we stopped relying on ourselves and learned to rely only on God.

2 CORINTHIANS 1:8—9 NLT

Dear Lord, strengthen me. Refresh me with Your Spirit.
Fill my heart with so much encouragement that it spills over,
splashing onto all those around me. Use me to build them up,
inspiring them to be all You made them to be, helping them
gather strength from trusting You. Amen. MJ

Encourage one another and build each other up, just as in fact you are doing.

1 THESSALONIANS 5:11 NIV

O Lord God, in whom we live, and move, and have our being, open our eyes that we may behold Your fatherly presence ever about us. Draw our hearts to You with the power of Your love.... Lift our thoughts up to You in heaven, and make us to know that all things are possible to us through Your Son, our Redeemer.

Brooke Foss Westcott

Steep yourself in God-reality, God-initiative, God-provisions.
You'll find all your everyday human concerns will be met....
You're my dearest friends! The Father wants to give you the very kingdom itself.

LUKE 12:31–32 MSG

Lord, protect me from temptation today. Strengthen me so I am able to say no! Help me to stand firm, even if I stand by myself. For I am never alone—You are always with me. Amen. MJ

God is faithful; he will not let you be tempted beyond what you can bear.
But when you are tempted, he will also provide a way out so that you can endure it.

1 CORINTHIANS 10:13 NIV

The prayer preceding all prayers is "May it be the real
I who speaks. May it be the real You that I speak to."

C. S. Lewis

The LORD is the true God; He is the living God and the everlasting King.

JEREMIAH 10:10 NASB

I will sing Your praises, O God Almighty. I will forever sing Your praises, even as they have been sung for generations and generations. Your Word is unchangeable, O God, it is as solid as the mountains. Amen. MJ

Great is the LORD, and greatly to be praised;
And His greatness is unsearchable.
One generation shall praise Your works to another,
And shall declare Your mighty acts.

PSALM 145:3–4 NKJV

O Lord, my God, grant us Your peace; already, indeed,
You have made us rich in all things! Give us that peace of being
at rest, that Sabbath peace, the peace which knows no end.

Augustine

May there be peace within your walls....
For the sake of my family and friends, I will say,
"May you have peace."

PSALM 122:7–8 NLT

*D*ear Jesus, at times it has been difficult, but I am fighting
the good fight. Through it all, I have kept the faith.
I may have wavered, but I have not quit.
Strengthen my faith so it wavers less and less. Amen. MJ

This is the only race worth running. I've run hard right to the finish,
believed all the way. All that's left now is the shouting!

2 TIMOTHY 4:7–8 MSG

I found the sun for me this morning. I thank You, Lord....
I found the fresh air as I stood outside the door. I praise You.
For all that I see that You do for me, I thank You.
For all that I do not see that You do for me, I praise You.

Christopher de Vinck

Rejoice always, pray continually, give thanks in all circumstances;
for this is God's will for you.

1 THESSALONIANS 5:16–18 NIV

Dear God, did I tell You I love You today? I do. I love You for just being You. I also love You for loving me. I love You for saving me, for providing for me, for protecting me, for forgiving me. You're awesome, God, marvelous and wonderful. Help me to glorify You in all I do. Amen. MJ

I love you, LORD; you are my strength.
The LORD is my rock, my fortress, and my savior;
my God is my rock, in whom I find protection.

PSALM 18:1–2 NLT

*L*ord Jesus, teach me to be generous…
to give and not to count the cost.

Ignatius Loyola

Now, our God, we give you thanks, and praise your glorious name. But who am I,
and who are my people, that we should be able to give as generously as this?
Everything comes from you, and we have given you only what comes from your hand.

1 CHRONICLES 29:13–14 NIV

*H*eavenly Father…whether we are two or ten in number,
thank You for the blessing of being a part of a family. Amen.

Kim Boyce

You've blessed my family so that it will continue in your presence always. Because you have blessed it, GOD, it's really blessed—blessed for good!

1 CHRONICLES 17:27 MSG

*L*ord, I want my life so consumed by Your love that others see and feel the difference. When people get close to me and know my heart, I pray they will see the real deal. Help me to be authentic about my faith.

Dan Britton and Jimmy Page

Their good character will shine through their actions,
adding luster to the teaching of our Savior God.

TITUS 2:10 MSG

Speak through the earthquake, wind, and fire,
O still, small voice of calm.

John Greenleaf Whittier

After the wind there was an earthquake, but the LORD was not in the earthquake.
After the earthquake came a fire, but the LORD was not in the fire.
And after the fire came a gentle whisper.

1 KINGS 19:11−12 NIV

Lord, please remove my fear and doubt. Turn my suffering into compassion, my weakness into strength, my sorrow into joy, and my pain into comfort. Help me to trust in Your goodness and hope in Your faithfulness. Amen. MJ

Their sorrow was turned into gladness and their mourning into joy.

ESTHER 9:22 NLT

God, enable us by Your wisdom to keep things in perspective.
For, God, You are bigger than the problems we face each day.

M. Y. Lee

In this world you will have trouble.
But take heart! I have overcome the world.

JOHN 16:33 NIV

I never cease to pray that God will guard and keep you safe
within His love each day.

Janie Harper Ford

The Lord is faithful, and he will strengthen you and protect you.

2 THESSALONIANS 3:3 NIV

You can talk to God because God listens.
Your voice matters in heaven. He takes you very seriously.
When you enter His presence, the attendants turn to you
to hear your voice. No need to fear that you will be ignored.
Even if you stammer or stumble, even if what you have to say
impresses no one, it impresses God—and He listens.

Max Lucado

I love the LORD because he hears my voice and my prayer....
Because he bends down to listen, I will pray as long as I have breath!

O the pure delight of a single hour
that before Your throne I spend,
When I kneel in prayer, and with You, my God,
I commune as friend with friend!

Fanny Crosby

You will call upon Me and go and pray to Me, and I will listen to you.
And you will seek Me and find Me, when you search for Me with all your heart.

Mighty God, Source of strength, I thank You for Your blessings. Only when walking with You do I find the courage and wisdom to go through each day. You fill my life with joy, providing everything I need. Amen MJ

Be strong. Take courage. Don't be intimidated. Don't give them a second thought because GOD, your God, is striding ahead of you. He's right there with you. He won't let you down; he won't leave you.

DEUTERONOMY 31:6 MSG

Accept, O Lord, our thanks and praise for all that You have done for us. We thank You for the splendor of the whole creation, for the beauty of this world, for the wonder of life, and for the mystery of love.

The Book of Common Prayer

*I will praise the name of God with song
And magnify Him with thanksgiving.*

PSALM 69:30 NASB

*D*earest God, help me to pray more. I forget sometimes
to ask You first before I do things or make decisions.
I want to share my life with You more. I need Your wisdom.
I need to hear Your voice. Please help me. Amen. MJ

If any of you lacks wisdom, you should ask God,
who gives generously to all without finding fault, and it will be given to you.

JAMES 1:5 NIV

God give me joy in the common things:
In the dawn that lures, the eve that sings....
God give me joy in the love of friends,
In the dear home talk as summer ends.

Thomas Curtis Clark

I pray that God, the source of hope, will fill you completely with joy and peace because you trust in him. Then you will overflow with confident hope through the power of the Holy Spirit.

ROMANS 15:13 NLT

Lord, I crave my moments of quiet. I need those times to have
real conversation with You. Still my soul. Please, Lord, give me time
to unburden my heart, to share with You the cries, the praises,
the frustrations, and the prayers for others. Amen. MJ

Quiet down before GOD, be prayerful before him.

PSALM 37:7 MSG

Father, Your daily giving is so often taken for granted.
Help me to receive every gift with gratefulness and use it fully,
never leaving any part unused or unappreciated. Lead me
to where my gifts are most needed. Help me to share all
I have and find more to give. Bless my gifts. Amen. MJ

Yes, you will be enriched in every way so that you can always be generous.
And when we take your gifts to those who need them, they will thank God.

2 CORINTHIANS 9:11 NLT

Use me then, my Savior, for whatever purposes,
and in whatever way you may require. Here is my poor heart,
an empty vessel; fill it with your grace.

D. L. Moody

[We] pray that our God will make you fit for what he's called you to be,
pray that he'll fill your good ideas and acts of faith with his own energy
so that it all amounts to something.

2 THESSALONIANS 1:11 MSG

Lord God, search my heart! Guide me! Still my tongue when it is getting out of control. Help me to quiet my emotions and lean on You. Amen. MJ

Search me, O God, and know my heart; test me and know my anxious thoughts.

PSALM 139:23 NLT

....

....

....

....

....

....

....

....

....

....

....

....

....

....

....

....

....

....

....

....

Calm me, O Lord, as You stilled the storm,
Still me, O Lord, keep me from harm.
Let all the tumult within me cease,
Enfold me, Lord, in Your peace.

Celtic Traditional

What a blessing was that stillness as he brought them safely into harbor! Let them praise the LORD for his great love and for the wonderful things he has done for them.

PSALM 107:30–31 NLT

Father, You have the power to overcome all. You conquer every trouble. Your strength always prevails. I praise You, Father, that through You, I also will prevail. Your strength is my strength and for that I am eternally grateful. Amen. MJ

God is our refuge and strength,
A very present help in trouble.
Therefore we will not fear.

PSALM 46:1–2 NASB

Speak, move, act in peace, as if you were in prayer.
In truth, this is prayer.

François de Fénelon

Dear children, let us not love with words or speech but with actions and in truth.

1 JOHN 3:18 NIV

Father in heaven, thank You for not giving up on me. All along You've kept patiently bringing me back to Your presence. Now I realize that next to You is where I want to be. Amen. MJ

Because of my integrity you uphold me and set me in your presence forever.
Praise be to the LORD, the God of Israel, from everlasting to everlasting.

PSALM 41:12–13 NIV

Allow your dreams a place in your prayers and plans.
God-given dreams can help you move into the future
He is preparing for you.

Barbara Johnson

God can do anything, you know—far more than you could ever imagine
or guess or request in your wildest dreams! He does it not by pushing us around
but by working within us, his Spirit deeply and gently within us.

EPHESIANS 3:20–21 MSG

Thank You, Father, for holding me steady when
I would rather run away. Give me not the easy path,
but the endurance to travel the difficult one. Amen. MJ

*Be strong and courageous. Do not be afraid or terrified...for the LORD your God
goes with you; he will never leave you nor forsake you.*

DEUTERONOMY 31:6 NIV

Thank You, Lord, for the bed sheets roused to life
in billowing winds, thank You for fluff of a sparrow landing
on [the] line, for wooden clothespins and sun winter warmth,
and one last leaf still hanging in the orchard.

Ann Voskamp

Since everything God created is good,
we should not reject any of it but receive it with thanks.

1 TIMOTHY 4:4 NLT

You are the great Overcomer. You have promised
that with Your help I can also be an overcomer.
You have promised a way through my troubles.
I cling to that promise right now. I believe in You. Amen. MJ

You...are from God and have overcome them [every spirit that does not acknowledge Jesus], because the one who is in you is greater than the one who is in the world.

1 JOHN 4:4 NIV

The highest form of prayer is to the goodness of God....
God only desires that our soul...clings to His goodness.
For of all the things our minds can think about God,
it is thinking about His goodness that pleases Him most
and brings the most profit to our soul.

Julian of Norwich

Your awe-inspiring deeds will be on every tongue;
I will proclaim your greatness.
Everyone will share the story of your wonderful goodness.

PSALM 145:6–7 NLT

Lord, remind me that You are the victor. Sometimes I forget that You are superior to the problems of my day, that You can turn my weakness into triumph. With Your help, I can persevere through any trouble. Thank You. Amen. MJ

For whatever is born of God overcomes the world.
And this is the victory that has overcome the world—our faith.

1 JOHN 5:4 NKJV

Disturb us, Lord, to dare more boldly,
To venture on wider seas
Where storms will show Your mastery;
Where losing sight of land,
We shall find the stars.

Sir Francis Drake

Lord, You are awesome. You refresh my soul. Your Word,
Your creation, the relationships You bring into my life
encourage my soul daily. You are my guiding light. Thank You.
Amen. MJ

Your word is a lamp to guide my feet and a light for my path.

PSALM 119:105 NLT

O my God, if Your creations are so full of beauty, delight, and joy, how infinitely more full of beauty, delight, and joy are You Yourself, Creator of all!

Nicodemus of the Holy Mountain

Who is like you among the gods, O LORD—glorious in holiness,
awesome in splendor, performing great wonders?

EXODUS 15:11 NLT

Lord, may the work of my hands—whatever that work may be—
bring glory to Your name. Thank You for the opportunity of it
and the skill to perform it. Thank You for the opening to serve
You in this area. Lord, please bless the work of my hands. Amen. MJ

Whatever you do, work at it with all your heart, as working for the Lord, not for human masters, since you know that you will receive an inheritance from the Lord as a reward. It is the Lord Christ you are serving.

COLOSSIANS 3:23–24 NIV

God specializes in things fresh and firsthand.
His plans for you this year may outshine those of the past....
He's preparing to fill your days with reasons to give Him praise.

Joni Eareckson Tada

LORD, you are my God; I will exalt you and praise your name, for in perfect faithfulness you have done wonderful things, things planned long ago.

ISAIAH 25:1 NIV

Lord, You are my guide. Because I have You, I have everything
I need. You lull me to sleep in gentle meadows. You give me
water from pure, bubbling streams. You refresh my soul.
You guide me to the right path. I'd be lost without You.

Prayer from Psalm 23

The LORD will guide you always;
he will satisfy your needs in a sun-scorched land.

ISAIAH 58:11 NIV

Come find me, Lord.
Be with me exactly as I am.
Help me find me, Lord.
Help me accept what I am
so I can begin to be Yours.

Ted Loder

This is what the Lord GOD says:
I, myself, will search for my sheep and take care of them.

EZEKIEL 34:11 NCV

Jesus, help me to be a faithful giver. When I have choices
of where to give, show me where You want me to give.
Teach me not to make decisions out of fear, but out of faithfulness,
cheerfulness, and thankfulness. Amen. MJ

Every good and perfect gift is from above, coming down from the Father of the heavenly lights, who does not change like shifting shadows.

JAMES 1:17 NIV

If there are any tears shed in heaven,
they will be over the fact that we prayed so little. Heaven is full
of answers to prayer for which no one ever bothered to ask.

Billy Graham

Ask and it will be given to you; seek and you will find; knock and the door will be opened to you. For everyone who asks receives; the one who seeks finds; and to the one who knocks, the door will be opened.

MATTHEW 7:7–8 NIV

Lord Jesus Christ, You are the source of all food,
material and spiritual, nourishing us in both body and soul.
You are the light that dispels the clouds of error and doubt.
May I walk in Your light, be nourished by Your food,
be sustained by Your mercy, and be warmed by Your love.

Desiderius Erasmus

The LORD is my light and my salvation;
Whom shall I fear?
THE LORD is the strength of my life;
Of whom shall I be afraid?

PSALM 27:1 NKJV

Dear Father, thank You for everything You've given me.
You surprise me all the time with just what I need right when
I need it. I love how You do that. Help me to trust You to supply
what is necessary. Thank You for being my Provider. Amen. MJ

God will generously provide all you need. Then you will always have everything you need and plenty left over to share with others.

2 CORINTHIANS 9:8 NLT

*D*o you know why the mighty God of the universe chooses
to answer prayer? It is because His children ask.
God delights in our asking. He is pleased at our asking.
His heart is warmed by our asking.

Richard J. Foster

I am praying to you because I know you will answer, O God.
Bend down and listen as I pray.
Show me your unfailing love in wonderful ways.

PSALM 17:6–7 NLT

Lord, I praise You. I magnify Your name. I am daily amazed by Your grace and mercy. You are the heart of my life. Without You my life would be incomplete. With You I have everything I need. I worship and praise Your name. Amen. MJ

Lord, our Lord, how majestic is your name in all the earth!
You have set your glory in the heavens.

PSALM 8:1 NIV

Slow me down, Lord.... Remind me each day
That the race is not always won by the fastest runner;
That there is more to life than increasing its speed.

Wilferd A. Peterson

The LORD's loved ones will lie down in safety,
because he protects them all day long.
The ones he loves rest with him

DEUTERONOMY 33:12 NCV

Forgive us if this day we have done or said anything to increase the pain of the world. Pardon the unkind word, the impatient gesture, the hard and selfish deed, the failure to show sympathy and kindly help where we had the opportunity, but missed it; and enable us so to live that we may daily do something to lessen the tide of human sorrow, and add to the sum of human happiness.

F. B. Meyer

*Be kind and compassionate to one another, forgiving each other,
just as in Christ God forgave you.*

EPHESIANS 4:32 NIV

Wait before the Lord. Wait in the stillness.
And in that stillness, assurance will come to you.

Amy Carmichael

Be still, and know that I am God.

PSALM 46:10 NIV

*H*eavenly Father, thank You for the opportunity to laugh.
Help me to find joy in everything that I do. Let me laugh
and be cheerful, so that those around me
will be blessed by my smile and my optimism. Amen.

Kim Boyce

Satisfy us in the morning with your unfailing love,
that we may sing for joy and be glad all our days.

PSALM 90:14 NIV

Thank You, Father, for putting me right where I am.
So many times I've heard "bloom where you are planted."
Help me to do that. Help me take whatever gifts and talents You
have given me and use them in my neighborhood. Help me
to spread Your love from where I am right now. Amen. MJ

Whatever job you're given to do, do it. God is with you!

1 SAMUEL 10:7 MSG

_____

_____

_____

_____

_____

_____

_____

_____

_____

_____

_____

_____

_____

_____

_____

_____

_____

_____

What God gives in answer to our prayers will always be the thing
we most urgently need, and it will always be sufficient.

Elisabeth Elliot

Your Father already knows your needs. Seek the Kingdom of God above all else,
and he will give you everything you need.

LUKE 12:30–31 NLT

Lord, I want a good, positive attitude in all areas of my life. Guard my thoughts and attitudes. Let thanksgiving and praise come easily to my lips. My hope is in You. Amen. MJ

The Kingdom of God is not a matter of what we eat or drink, but of living a life of goodness and peace and joy in the Holy Spirit. If you serve Christ with this attitude, you will please God, and others will approve of you, too.

ROMANS 14:17–18 NLT

So this is my prayer: that your love will flourish and that you will not only love much but well. Learn to love appropriately. You need to use your head and test your feelings so that your love is sincere and intelligent, not sentimental gush. Live a lover's life, circumspect and exemplary, a life Jesus will be proud of: bountiful in fruits from the soul.

Philippians 1:9–11 MSG

These three remain: faith, hope and love. But the greatest of these is love.

1 CORINTHIANS 13:13 NIV

O God, Father of all, help us to forgive others as we would wish them to forgive us…. May we see with their eyes, think with their minds, feel with their hearts. Then let us ask ourselves whether we should judge them, or judge ourselves and accept them as children, like us, of one heavenly Father.

William Barclay

Clothe yourselves with compassion, kindness, humility, gentleness and patience.
Bear with each other and forgive one another if any of you has a grievance
against someone. Forgive as the Lord forgave you.

COLOSSIANS 3:12–13 NIV

Dearest Creator of all things, I praise Your name.
I praise Your creativity in making such a wondrous world.
Just thinking of how all things on earth come together in
such glorious harmonies is amazing. I don't have the words to
adequately tell You how truly spectacular Your creation is to me.
You are worthy of all praise. Amen. MJ

You are worthy, our Lord and God, to receive glory and honor and power,
for you created all things, and by your will they were created and have their being.

REVELATION 4:11 NIV

Let the healing grace of Your love, O Lord, so transform me that
I may play my part in the transfiguration of the world from a place
of suffering, death, and corruption to a realm of infinite light,
joy, and love. Make me so obedient to Your Spirit that my life may
become a living prayer, and a witness to Your unfailing presence.

Martin Israel

Nothing [is] between us and God, our faces shining with the brightness of his face. And so we are transfigured...our lives gradually becoming brighter and more beautiful as God enters our lives and we become like him.

2 CORINTHIANS 3:18 MSG

Give me grace today, O Lord. Help me to be merciful to those who need mercy. Help me to be kind to those who need kindness. Help me to be gentle with those who need gentleness. Help me to be generous with those who need generosity. Help me to be more like You. Amen. MJ

You know the grace of our Lord Jesus Christ, that though he was rich, yet for your
sake he became poor, so that you through his poverty might become rich.

2 CORINTHIANS 8:9 NIV

God be in my head, and in my understanding;
God be in my eyes, and in my looking;
God be in my mouth, and in my speaking;
God be in my heart, and in my thinking;
God be at my end, and at my departing.

Sarum Primer

Worship and serve [God] with your whole heart and a willing mind.
For the LORD sees every heart and knows every plan and thought.
If you seek him, you will find him.

1 CHRONICLES 28:9 NLT

O Lord, thank You for being my strength when I am weak.
When I feel sad and lonely and I call on Your name,
You come and fill me with Your love. Your promise to never
leave my side helps keep me near You. Amen. MJ

I will bless the LORD who guides me;
even at night my heart instructs me.
I know the LORD is always with me.
I will not be shaken, for he is right beside me.

PSALM 16:7–8 NLT

A joyful heart is like a sunshine of God's love, the hope of
eternal happiness, a burning flame of God. And if we pray,
we will become that sunshine of God's love—in our own home,
the place where we live, and in the world at large.

Mother Teresa

Because of the tender mercy of our God…the Sunrise from on high will visit us…
to guide our feet into the way of peace.

LUKE 1:78–79 NASB

Dear Lord, shine through me, and be so evident in me that every soul I come in contact with may feel Your presence in my soul.... Let me thus praise You in the way You love best, by shining on those around me. Amen. MJ

GOD, you floodlight my life;
I'm blazing with glory, God's glory!

PSALM 18:28 MSG

*L*ord, Your Word is full of knowledge and wisdom.
It has answers to questions I haven't yet thought to ask.
It is a map for my journey through life.
Thank You for the gift of it. Amen. MJ

Guide me down the road of your commandments;
I love traveling this freeway.... What you say is always so good.

PSALM 119:35, 39 MSG

Prayer, to be prayer, to have any power to change anything, must first speak thanks.

Ann Voskamp

In everything, by prayer and petition, with thanksgiving,
present your requests to God.

PHILIPPIANS 4:6 NIV

Lord, I trust that no matter where my path leads,
You will be there before me. You are here, there, everywhere—
even on the far side of the sea. I pray that You will help
me accept the changes that come, that You will fill me with
contentment in every situation and every location. Amen. MJ

If I rise on the wings of the dawn,
if I settle on the far side of the sea,
even there your hand will guide me,
your right hand will hold me fast.

PSALM 139:9–10 NIV

We desire many things and [God] offers us only one thing.
He can offer us only one thing—Himself. He has nothing
else to give. There is nothing else to give.

Peter Kreeft

Whom have I in heaven but You?
And besides You, I desire nothing on earth.
My flesh and my heart may fail,
But God is the strength of my heart and my portion forever.

PSALM 73:25–26 NASB

*D*ear Lord, grant me the grace of wonder. Surprise me,
amaze me, awe me in every crevice of Your universe.
Delight me…. Each day enrapture me with Your marvelous
things without number. I do not ask to see the reason for it all;
I ask only to share the wonder of it all.

Abraham Joshua Heschel